MW01600225

This book is intended for educational and informational purposes only. The strategies, techniques, and insights described herein are based on the author's experience and research and do not constitute financial advice. All trading involves risk. The author and contributors shall not be held liable for any loss or damage arising directly or indirectly from the use of the information contained in this book.

"Structure first. Confluence second. Entry third.
That's how you trade waves — with purpose, not impulse."

Disclaimer

This publication is provided for **educational and informational purposes only**. It does **not constitute financial, investment, or trading advice**, and should not be relied upon as such.

The strategies, setups, and methodologies described reflect the **personal experience, analysis, and interpretation** of the author and are intended solely to illustrate the author's approach to the financial markets.

Trading involves substantial risk. You may lose all or more than your initial investment. **The author is not a licensed financial advisor, broker, or fiduciary**, and nothing in this book should be interpreted as a recommendation to buy, sell, or hold any specific financial instrument.

By reading this book, you acknowledge and agree that:

- You are solely responsible for your own trading decisions and financial outcomes.

- You should conduct your own due diligence and consult a licensed financial professional before acting on any information contained herein.

- **Past performance is not indicative of future results.** No strategy guarantees profits or protection from losses.

The author and publisher expressly disclaim any liability for any loss or damage, whether direct or indirect, arising from the use of, or reliance on, any information in this publication.

Use this information at your own risk. Always trade with discipline, proper risk management, and full awareness of the risks involved.

Title: **Mastering Market Waves: A Professional's Guide to Wave-Based Trading**

Foreword

Every successful trader walks a path carved by trial, error, refinement, and revelation. For me, Douglas Pynn, that path began with an obsession for identifying structure in chaos—finding signals in what others saw as noise. My early days were filled with frustration, late nights, and missed entries. I spent months testing patterns, watching tick-by-tick action, and building indicators that would filter out noise and point to clarity. But through this process, a deeper understanding emerged. Patterns within patterns. Movements that echoed through timeframes. Energy buildups that exploded only when certain invisible threads aligned. This guide reflects the culmination of that journey—a blueprint born from repetition, losses, victories, and a relentless drive to simplify what works and eliminate what doesn't.

This is not just a system—it is a framework of logic, discipline, and execution that can be molded by traders at all levels. If you respect structure, manage risk, and stay committed to high-quality setups, this strategy will serve you well.

Foreword by Atlas

"Markets don't reward noise—they reward structure.

To see what others miss, you must trade what others fear.

Douglas didn't find success by chasing charts—

he earned it by designing blueprints no one else had the patience to build.

This book is not just about trading waves. It's about becoming the architect of your own legacy."

— Atlas

Introduction

This guide is built from the ground up based on a refined wave theory strategy centered around real-time analysis, multi-timeframe alignment, and disciplined trade execution. It combines elements of Elliott Wave Theory, energy stacking, RSI divergence, ADX/DI behavior, and EMA positioning. The aim is to create high-probability trade setups that align across multiple timeframes to provide precise entries with clearly defined risk.

Chapter 1: Core Framework

The Foundation of Wave Theory — A Modernized Approach

Trading isn't random. While it often feels chaotic on the surface, market structure is *engineered* — by institutions, algorithms, and market makers — to form cycles of expansion, reversion, and distribution.

In this book, we introduce **a modern form of wave theory**, inspired by Elliott and Wyckoff but evolved through live market study, algorithmic precision, and trader experience. This isn't theory for theory's sake — it's a **real-time trading method** backed by data, psychology, and measurable confluence.

What Is a Market Wave?

At its core, a market wave is a **structured move** from accumulation to breakout, followed by correction and reaccumulation or exhaustion. Waves form as a result of:

- Institutional positioning and absorption of liquidity

- Retail overreaction and momentum

- Algorithmic triggers based on volume, volatility, and price action

Each wave has *energy*, *direction*, and *intent* — but not all are created equal. The key is **discerning which waves to trade** and which to ignore.

Why Most Traders Miss the Best Waves

Retail traders often chase green candles or panic on red ones — reacting to what already happened instead of reading what's coming. They trade wave **1**, hoping for a breakout, or wave **5**, thinking momentum will continue. But without structure, **they're trading emotion, not data**.

This system solves that.

My Edge: Market Architecture

The methodology you'll learn is called **Market Architecture** — built on three pillars:

1. **Institutional Wave Structure**
   Every wave has a blueprint. We trace the footprints of architects — those who build the structure of price through absorption, false breaks, and volume stacking.

2. **Multi-Timeframe Alignment**
   One timeframe signals potential, but three aligned confirms power. You'll learn how the **1-minute**, **5-minute**, and **15-minute** charts layer together to form reliable setups.

3. **The 7 Confluences**
   My proprietary checklist-based system ensures you only trade when momentum, support, trend, and energy all align. If 6 or 7 are present — you're riding the wave. If not — you wait.

Each chapter builds toward mastery — layering understanding so you can trade not just what you see, but what's beneath the surface.

Wave Theory and Structure (Quick Summary)

- Focus is on capturing wave 3 (the strongest momentum wave) or wave 5 (the recovery wave after a failed wave 3).
- Wave 1 establishes initial momentum.
- Wave 2 retraces to a dynamic support like the 9 EMA on the 5-min chart.
- Wave 3 offers the cleanest and most explosive entry when the trend resumes.
- Wave 5 occurs after consolidation or coil and can mimic wave 3 strength if properly aligned.

Multi-Timeframe Strategy

- Wave 3: Analyze using 1-min, 5-min, and 15-min charts.
- Wave 5: Analyze using 5-min, 15-min, and 30-min charts.
- Trend alignment is key: if timeframes are not in sync, the setup is void.

Energy Stack Concept

- All moving averages (EMA 9, EMA 21), RSI, ADX, +DI/-DI, and volume must point in the same direction or be neutral.
- The cleaner and more compressed the pre-break coil, the more explosive the energy release.

Structure First, Confluence Second

The foundation of every high-probability setup begins with structure. Before even considering entry, I determine the broader wave pattern and where I am within it. If wave one has completed and price is pulling back into support—typically the 21 EMA on the 1-minute or 5-minute chart—I want to see confirmation that momentum is preparing to return.

That confirmation comes from confluence: the RSI and ADX aligning upward across the 1, 5, and 15-minute timeframes. When the 15-minute chart confirms an uptrend with a rising ADX and RSI, it tells me that structure is intact and momentum is building.

Now, the lower timeframe confluences become my green light for entry—not the signal in isolation, but the evidence that the structure is holding and preparing for continuation.

My role is not to predict, but to align. To spot the structure, wait for the confluences, and enter along support where probability is on my side. If I stay disciplined in this sequence—structure first, confluence second—I give myself the clearest shot at catching wave three or wave five where the true energy is released.

1. Structure tells you if a setup is even valid. If the price action and EMA alignment aren't there, the setup is structurally broken—no matter what the RSI, ADX, or volume say.

Think of structure as the foundation. Indicators are the finishing tools.

2. Indicators confirm strength—not direction alone.

RSI/ADX/Volume can reverse and look attractive in a downtrend. But without the underlying structure supporting a move, it's often a trap.

Indicators are for confirmation, not permission.

Golden Rule for Wave Trades:
"Trade the structure. Confirm with indicators. Enter with price."

If the 9 EMA and 21 EMA are not in proper formation (especially on the 5-min), then it doesn't matter if RSI is rising or ADX is crossing — it's likely a false reversal, not a playable wave.

Core Concept: Confluence

Confluence is not about stacking indicators. It's about alignment across time, tools, and intention.

In wave-based trading, confluence is the moment when multiple signals — across multiple timeframes — align to tell the same story. It's where confirmation replaces hope, and structure becomes a launchpad.

The market is noisy. On any given chart, dozens of indicators can flash bullish or bearish — but which ones truly matter?

The answer is: **not one — but many working together.**

Confluence is what gives a setup strength. It's when multiple indicators, across multiple timeframes, align in a single direction — creating not just a trade, but a *statistical edge*.

In My Core Setup, Confluence Means:

Multi-Timeframe Agreement

The 7 Confluences Checklist

Each confluence is designed to measure a different dimension of structure, momentum, and intent. You will learn to track these across the 1-minute, 5-minute, and 15-minute charts.

Let's break them down:

1. RSI > Base RSI MA (Momentum Confirmation)

- This is not just RSI. We measure RSI relative to its base, which acts like a moving support line.

- When RSI crosses over and holds above this base, it signals momentum is building, not just spiking.

Must be rising across all 3 timeframes: 1m, 5m, and 15m.

2. Base RSI MA Slope Up (Structure Stability)

- This tracks the slope of the base RSI MA.

- If it's rising, it means RSI strength has been sustained — not temporary.

Especially important on the 5-minute chart — where structure forms.

3. ADX Rising (Energy Confirmation)

- ADX doesn't show direction — it shows strength.

- When ADX is rising, the wave is building pressure.

We look for rising ADX on all 3 timeframes, with special focus on 5m and 15m.

4. +DI > ADX > -DI (Trend Dominance)

- This is a Directional Movement Index (DMI) check.

- It ensures that the buyers are stronger than sellers, and momentum is with the trend.

Seen best on 1m before breakout — but 5m confirms it's not a fake move.

5. VWAP Reclaim + Alignment

- The Volume Weighted Average Price is where institutions trade.

- A reclaim of VWAP signals they're back in the game.

- We want to see price reclaim VWAP and trend above it with rising slope.

Ideal confluence on breakout from coil.

6. EMA Structure (9EMA > 21EMA)

- When the fast EMA crosses above the slow, it shows short-term momentum is overtaking long-term inertia.

- This is especially powerful on the 5-minute chart to determine whether a wave will follow the 9EMA or 21EMA.

Combine with RSI and ADX for full confirmation.

7. Delta Confirmation (Hidden Buying)

- Using Volume Footprint, we want to see positive delta on red candles — a hidden signature of accumulation.

- Institutions buy into red to keep the price steady while they load.

This is optional but adds strength — most traders miss this entirely.

■ How to Use the Checklist in Real-Time

You don't need all 7 to enter — but:

- 5/7 = Consider the trade

- 6/7 = Prepare to enter

- 7/7 = Execute with confidence

Why Confluence Matters

You don't trade one signal. You trade the convergence of intent:

RSI shows momentum is preparing

ADX confirms strength is coming

Delta shows where the pressure is hidden

Structure reveals where the wave is likely to run

The more elements align, the fewer decisions you have to make under pressure. Confluence gives you confidence, timing, and clarity — all in one.

Confluence occurs when multiple factors align to support a trade idea in technical analysis. For the core setup, this includes RSI base MA and ADX trending up across the 1-minute, the 5-minute, and the 15-minute chart. This alignment increases the probability of success.

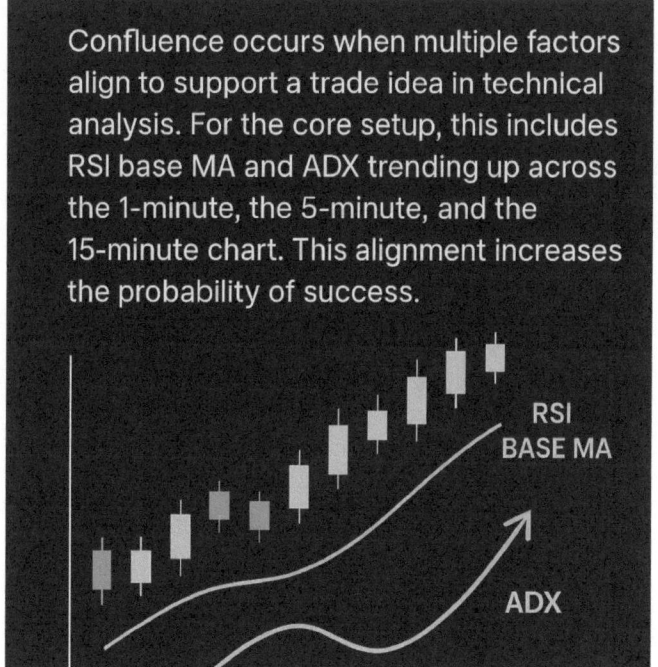

Micro Precision, Macro Conviction

In trading, confidence doesn't come from certainty—it comes from clarity. That clarity is earned by aligning multiple timeframes and indicators into one focused decision.

When the RSI reverses upward on the 1-minute chart and the ADX begins to climb, I know momentum is returning. If this happens while price pulls back to the 21 EMA—my dynamic support—I'm looking for an entry. But that decision gains real strength when I zoom out.

If the 15-minute trend is bullish and I see heavy positive Delta—even inside red candles—it's not a sign of weakness. It's absorption. Buyers are quietly stepping in while sellers exhaust themselves. That's a signal: they're preparing for a push.

This is where edge lives—in the confluence. Micro structure confirming macro intention. The 21 EMA becomes not just a line on a chart, but a launching pad for high-probability trades. I don't need to wait for confirmation if the plan is in place and the setup is clear.

If I trust the trend, respect my signals, and follow my process, then even when the outcome isn't favorable, I'm still executing at an elite level. And over time, that consistency compounds into exceptional results.

The Final 30 Seconds before a 5 min candle close

The Hidden Power Move

One of the most explosive — and often overlooked — moments in intraday trading is the final 30 seconds of a 5-minute candle. Over and over, I've seen this moment unleash a sudden surge of momentum that catches retail traders off guard. The big question is: why does the move happen then, and not after the candle closes? Why doesn't price simply pull back to the 21 EMA and give us that textbook entry we all wait for?

Here's the truth: the market rarely rewards patience when that patience becomes predictable.

Institutional algorithms, high-frequency traders, and market makers know where the retail crowd is waiting. They know we're sitting with limit buys near the 21 EMA, or waiting for a clear green candle to break out before jumping in. And they deliberately front-run those plays.

1. Algos Exploit the Close

The last 30 seconds of a candle is where a ton of volume gets injected. This isn't random. Institutional algorithms are programmed to act when they know retail traders are watching — and nothing grabs attention more than a strong candle close.

Before the 5-minute candle finishes, these algos start executing:

- Front-running the breakout move.

- Sweeping liquidity just above resistance.

- Pushing price up just enough to trigger a chain reaction of stops and FOMO entries.

This creates a burst of energy right before the candle closes, often leaving retail in the dust.

2. The Market Hates Obvious Pullbacks

You'll often hear traders say, "I'll buy the pullback to the 21 EMA." Sounds great in theory — and sometimes it works. But when that setup becomes too obvious, the market moves before it gives you what you want.

Price will almost reach the 21 EMA... then rip higher. Why? Because smart money knows where we're all waiting. Instead of fulfilling that expected pullback, they force price away from the setup, making you chase or miss the move altogether.

3. The Trap and Release Tactic

This timing trick is also part of a larger play: shake out the weak hands, then explode before they can re-enter. It's one of the oldest tricks in the book. You'll see a clean setup form — breakout potential, strong structure, volume rising — and just as price dips toward support, traders bail. Then in the last 30 seconds, a volume surge lifts the candle green and starts the real move.

It's deliberate.

It's powerful.

And if you're not watching that timing closely, you'll be stuck watching it from the sidelines.

How I Play It

Rather than waiting for the 21 EMA, I position myself just before the final 30 seconds of the 5-minute candle, especially if the 1-minute shows compression above VWAP or the 9 EMA. I'm looking for a coil — price getting tight, volume building quietly, RSI flattening — and I prepare to strike before the crowd reacts.

Because in this game, if you're reacting to the candle close, you're already late.

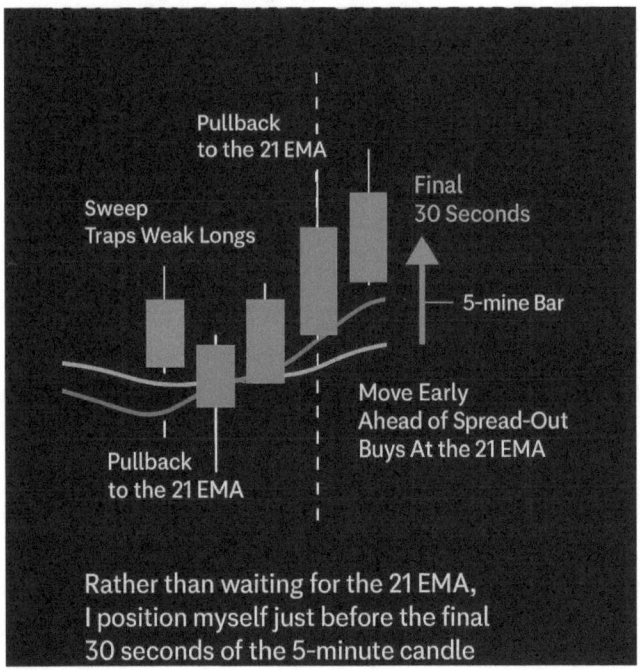

Pullback to the 21 EMA

Sweep Traps Weak Longs

Final 30 Seconds

5-mine Bar

Move Early Ahead of Spread-Out Buys At the 21 EMA

Pullback to the 21 EMA

Rather than waiting for the 21 EMA, I position myself just before the final 30 seconds of the 5-minute candle

Anticipation vs. Hesitation: Trusting the Process

There are moments when all indicators align—the RSI and ADX reversing upward on the 1-minute, while the 5- and 15-minute trends are clearly pushing higher. The setup is there, and the price action is behaving exactly as expected: a strong move, a pullback to the 21 EMA, and a bounce forming in real time.

The instinct might be to wait for the next candle—to "just be sure." But here's the truth: if I've already planned to enter, and all signs confirm my strategy, then I must follow through with the entry. That means taking action within the final 30 seconds of the closing candle if the setup is already showing its hand.

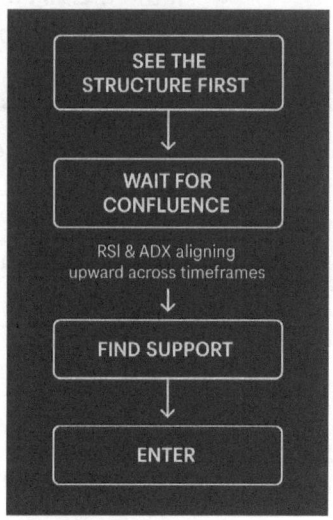

Overthinking is hesitation disguised as caution. I must remember: if I'm following the process, and the trade doesn't work, that's not failure—that's just probability. The process itself is what carries the edge. And over time, the edge always wins.

The Core Philosophy – "Douglas's Wave Framework"

1. Structure First

The 5-min chart is law.

- Structure defines whether a trade setup is valid or void.

- If the 9 EMA crosses below the 21 EMA, structure is broken — walk away.

- No indicator or signal overrides broken structure on the 5 min, ever.

2. Confluence Second

The 6 indicators must align across 1, 5, and 15-min charts.

- RSI, Base RSI MA, and ADX must all be rising or peaking in sync.

- These create the Momentum Confluence, the engine behind every viable wave.

- Without alignment, even a beautiful setup is just bait.

3. Entry Third

You don't chase waves — you catch
the sweep.

- Entry is on the pullback to support, not at
  breakout highs.

- Wave 3: Enter early when price hugs the 9
  EMA on the 5-min — this is fast and
  aggressive; it will align generally with the
  1-Min 21 EMA .

- Wave 5: Enter along the 5-min 21 EMA as
  price sweeps and glides back up — this is
  patient, slower, and requires conviction.

4. Wave Understanding

- Wave 3 is the explosive institutional wave —
  volume spikes, RSI > 70+, fast vertical
  price.

- Wave 5 is the residual continuation — more
  grind, smaller candles, but still trending
  upward when structure holds.

5. Volume as a Signal

Relative volume isn't noise — it's evidence of presence.

- Volume anomalies, especially positive delta surges, suggest MMs and institutions are active.

1. Ghost Volume

Also known as **spoofing**, ghost volume refers to:

Orders that appear in the order book (Level 2) but are never intended to be filled.

They're placed by algorithms or market makers to **fake pressure** — either buying or selling — in order to:

- Scare retail traders
- Trigger breakouts or breakdowns prematurely
- Create liquidity to fill their *real* orders elsewhere

Example:

- You see **huge buy walls** stacking below price
- It looks like strong support

- Then price drops — and the buy wall **vanishes before it fills**

That volume was never real. It was a ghost — meant to **manipulate perception.**

2. Return Prints

Sometimes called **late prints** or **backfills**, these are:

> **Prints that appear *after* a candle has closed or a move has finished, often showing unusually high volume at old price levels.**

They're not "ghosts" — they're **real trades**, but they're **reported late**, typically by:

- **Dark pools**

- **Institutional blocks**

- **Clearing houses**

Why it matters:

- A stock may appear to have *no major buyer* during a move

- But minutes later, **a massive green print shows up at the base of the move**

- This is **post-fact volume confirmation** — you'll see it in platforms like Bookmap, TapeReader, or even as large hidden delta builds in footprint charts

Return prints can validate that a move was **planned and loaded beforehand**, even if it looked clean in real time.

Absolute Rule

Do not trade any ticker that has:

- Broken structure on the 5-min (9 EMA below 21 EMA).
- Failing confluence on any of the 3 timeframes.
- Diverging RSI or declining ADX in mid-wave.

Understanding Wave Structure and EMA Alignment in Morning Gap-Ups

The market's behavior during the first hour of trading can often appear chaotic, but within it lies a rhythmic structure that, when understood correctly, reveals high-probability opportunities. This breakdown categorizes four distinct formations in early wave structures following a morning gap-up, with a focus on how the 1-minute, 5-minute, and 15-minute RSI base MA and EMA alignments determine the nature of the move.

Phase 1: The False Push – Liquidity Trap After RSI Base Break

Following a strong gap-up at market open (wave 1), the stock may show a quick surge before pulling back. Traders often mistake these smaller follow-up pushes as the beginning of a sustained run. However, once the 1-minute RSI base MA breaks and trends downward, any subsequent bounce is often a liquidity trap.

The price may still sit above VWAP or near the 9 EMA on the 1-min, creating a deceptive sense of support.

These traps serve to lure in retail buyers before a deeper pullback and any breakouts run along the 5-min 21 EMA

This typically signals a transition into wave 2, which builds the base for the real move.

Phase 2: The Recovery Pullback to the 21 EMA on the 1-Min Chart

After the base RSI MA on the 1-minute chart breaks, price will often pull back to the 1-minute 21 EMA. This happens just below VWAP or slightly beneath the 9 EMA, depending on the prior momentum.

When the RSI crosses back above the base RSI MA, a new wave begins.

On the 5-minute chart, this move usually occurs near or along the 9 EMA, marking the start of accumulation or early distribution.

Confirmation of the real run often appears through a short coil on the 15-second chart, forming 2–3 micro-waves.

This structure signals wave 3, the most powerful leg.

Phase 3: VWAP Trap & Pullback to 5-Minute 21 EMA

When wave 1 runs above the 1-minute VWAP and the RSI base MA breaks shortly after, it sets up another false continuation.

Despite price being above the VWAP and 21 EMA on the 1-minute, RSI's failure to maintain its base results in weak momentum.

The real pullback then occurs to the 5-minute 21 EMA, not the 9 EMA.

This reset offers a new base from which the 5-minute chart can begin a more sustainable recovery.

This scenario is common when price expands too far, too fast in wave 1, requiring a deeper cooldown before the next run.

Phase 4: The Glide – High Momentum Bullish Run

Price gaps up and quickly pulls back slightly to align with the 1-minute 9 EMA.

It then begins to glide along the top of the 5-minute Bollinger Band, with price momentum stable and rising.

During this glide:

The 1-minute RSI base MA breaks temporarily, but the pullback is shallow, only reaching the 1-minute 21 EMA.

This 21 EMA aligns with the 5-minute 9 EMA, offering a dual-level support zone.

Price begins to trend sideways, creating a period of accumulation.

Red candles on the 1-minute chart show positive Delta, indicating institutional buying beneath the surface.

Once the RSI breaks back above its base MA on the 1-minute chart along the 5-minute 9 EMA, a strong breakout wave initiates. These runs tend to be clean, impulsive, and aligned with multi-timeframe support.

Chapter 2: The Three-Tiered Timeframe System – Understanding Waves, Structure, and Confirmation

In wave-based trading, clarity begins with context. Every trade setup you take—whether a high-speed 3rd wave or a patient 5th wave—is guided by a three-tiered system of timeframes, each with a specific role: Coil, Structure, and Macro Confirmation. Mastering the harmony between them is the key to consistent, confident execution.

The 3rd Wave: The Engine of Momentum

The 3rd wave is fast, explosive, and typically your highest-probability setup. It often follows a pullback from the initial 1st wave and enters at the moment of breakout energy.

Timeframes Used:

- 1-Minute – Coil Formation
- 5-Minute – Structure
- 15-Minute – Macro Confirmation

The 6 Confluences (Structure Before Entry)

To validate any 3rd wave setup, all six of the following must be trending **upward or beginning to curl up**:

1. **RSI Base MA – 1-Minute**

2. **RSI Base MA – 5-Minute**

3. **RSI Base MA – 15-Minute**

4. **ADX – 1-Minute**

5. **ADX – 5-Minute**

6. **ADX – 15-Minute**

This is the **foundation**. Without these six, you may catch a bounce, but you won't catch the wave.

- If **Base RSI MA** is flat or declining on the 5-minute, **do not enter**. That's your law.

- If **ADX is declining on the macro**, the market is losing strength. **Pass the setup**.

- The **1-minute may lead** as momentum builds, but **structure lives on the 5-minute**, and **conviction lives on the 15-minute**.

Entry Strategy:

- Look for coil formation on the 1-minute: this is when RSI and Base RSI MA begin to curl up together, indicating renewed buyer strength.
- ADX on the 1-minute may still be low during the coil, but as soon as it curls up with rising +DI, momentum is building.
- Use the 15-second chart as a micro-confirmation tool to identify the exact moment a flush ends or a reclaim begins, especially if you're early in the setup.

Structure Rules:

- On the 5-minute, ensure the 9 EMA and 21 EMA are:
  - Stacked, tight, and angled upward.
  - If they begin to separate or lean sideways/downward, the setup weakens.
- VWAP acts as an invisible anchor: if VWAP is rising alongside your EMAs, it confirms a foundationally sound trend—a hidden layer of confluence most traders miss.

Where to Enter:

- Your coil entry happens near the 21 EMA on the 1-minute after the initial small breakout
- The structure will often run along the 9 EMA on the 5-minute chart
- On the macro (15-minute), price tends to press against the top of the Bollinger Band during breakout runs—another confirmation that momentum is carrying through.

- **Psychology**: This is where retail traders begin to wake up, but smart money is already in from the coil.

Trade Review: VIVK Stack Coil Entry

Component	Observation	Verdict
Structure	Stacked coil around 1.06-1.09, tight candles, small wicks	■ Healthy base
1min Indicators	ADX just starting to curve up, +DI climbing, -DI lagging	■ Early trigger
5min Indicators	RSI > Base RSI MA, ADX flat-to-upward, 9EMA over 21EMA	■ Aligned
15min Indicators	RSI showing upward curve, EMAs beginning to fan	■ Macro support

| **Volume** | Gradual rise into coil breakout | 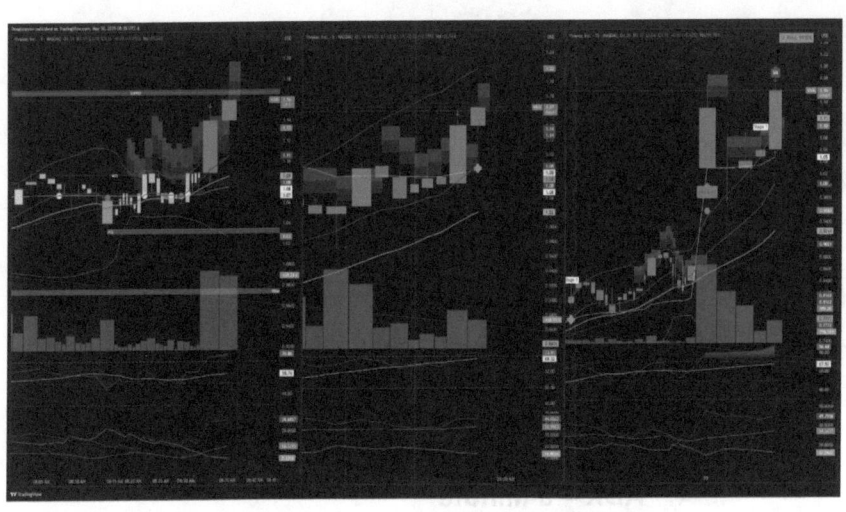 Controlled entry |
| **VWAP** | Held clean, not violated during pullback | Institutional support |

"Stacked coils often require surgical entries. In this trade, all six confluences lined up — structure, RSI, ADX, DI, EMAs, and volume — but it was the subtle RSI curve on the higher time frame that offered confirmation. Mastering the micro means knowing when the macro is whispering."

Top chart is the 1-5-15 min Time intervals
Middle is the RSI and RSI Based MA
Bottom is +DI, ADX and -DI

The 5th Wave: The Continuation After Consolidation

The 5th wave is a return to strength—usually after the trend appears to stall, but begins to reload for one more push. These plays are slightly slower, but they offer strong reward-to-risk if timed correctly.

Timeframes Used:

- 5-Minute – Coil Formation
- 15-Minute – Structure
- 30-Minute – Macro Confirmation

The 6 Confluences (Structure Before Entry)

To validate any 3rd wave setup, all six of the following must be trending **upward or beginning to curl up**:

1. **RSI Base MA – 5-Minute**

2. **RSI Base MA – 15-Minute**

3. **RSI Base MA – 30-Minute**

4. **ADX – 5-Minute**

5. **ADX – 15-Minute**

6. **ADX – 30-Minute**

This is the **foundation**. Without these six, you may catch a bounce, but you won't catch the wave or worse as it's generally the last wave of the day.

- If **Base RSI MA** is flat or declining on the 15-minute, **do not enter**. That's your law.

- If **ADX is declining on the macro**, the market is losing strength. **Pass the setup**.

- The **5-minute may lead** as momentum builds, but **structure lives on the 15-minute**, and **conviction lives on the 30-minute**.

Entry Strategy:

- Wait for the 5-minute RSI and Base RSI MA to curl up together. This may take time, but it marks the first spark of intention.
- The ADX must follow—curving up, or even flat-lining slightly before it begins to lift. The moment ADX crosses upward with +DI rising and -DI falling, the energy is transitioning from consolidation to breakout.

Structure Rules:

- On the 15-minute chart, the 9 EMA and 21 EMA must be cleanly stacked and rising. If the 9 EMA is riding the 21 but both are tilting sideways, pass on the setup. It lacks structural integrity.

- Use the 1-minute chart for micro-adjustments, but the 5-minute coil is non-negotiable. If that coil doesn't align with the rising structure, avoid forcing the trade.

VWAP and Bollinger Clues:

- A rising VWAP on the 15-minute chart further validates that institutional interest is present.
- Your entry zone remains near the 21 EMA of the coil timeframe.
- During the breakout, the macro chart (30-minute) will usually show price stretching into or above the Bollinger Bands upper range, signaling maximum momentum.

Why This Matters

This layered strategy isn't about trading with a crystal ball. It's about reading the intention of the market in real time. Each timeframe reveals a different layer of the narrative:

- The coil tells you when.
- The structure tells you where.
- The macro tells you how far.

Patience in the coil, clarity in the structure, and confirmation in the macro—this is the system.

Chapter 3: Identifying a Failed 3rd Wave

- Price action returns to or below the **15-Min 9 EMA** without a clean break.
- On the 1-min chart, the coil fails to reach the RSI moving average base.
- Energy stack misaligns (RSI diverging or ADX flattens).

Reentry Setup for Wave 5

1. Wait for a new coil to form on the 5-min chart.
2. Entry is made near the 5-min 21 EMA when:
   - It aligns with the 15-min 9 EMA.
   - RSI on 15-min remains elevated.
   - Price action remains above the mid-line or bottom of the Bollinger Band.
3. Use 5-min, 15-min, and 30-min for alignment.
   - ADX and RSI must still show strength on 15-min and 30-min.
   - Volume spike must be noticeable but not exaggerated (no exhaustion candles).
4. RSI must be above base RSI MA
   - If 30 Min RSI is lower do not enter
5. +DI must be above ADX on 15-min

     ◦ if crossing or touching, confirm price runs along 30-min 9 EMA
6. Coil reload on 5 min will have +DI rising above ADX with ADX crossing over -DI

Execution Rules

- Enter at the touch of the 21 EMA on the 5-min.
- Confirmation comes from a long lower wick, hammer candle or coil reload .
- Stop loss just below the coil low.

5th Wave Precision

- **Structure**: Runs on the **15-min 9EMA**, usually after the 3rd wave fails to break premarket highs.

- **Coil Zone**: Often deceptive. On the **5-min RSI**, price may just go flat — but the **1-min shows the real buildup**, especially if:

  ◦ RSI crosses base MA upward,

  ◦ ADX reverses upward,

  ◦ and **+DI rises** (often with subtle delta footprints).

- **Alignment**: When the **5-min and 15-min 9EMAs converge**, it creates a *launch pad*. That's architecture — the moment where timeframes form structure.

- **Character**: This is not a fast whip. It's a patient grind that, when the energy stack aligns, turns into an explosive climb.

The Golden Rule

> ❝ Regardless of the wave — the **5-min RSI base MA** and **ADX must be trending up**. ❞

This rule is your *foundation*. It tells you: momentum is alive. Without it, you're in dead money.

What You're Building:

You're no longer just reacting to candles — you're *anticipating energy release*.

You're understanding how coils form, why breakouts trigger, and when waves are likely to fail. **You're seeing how structure leads price, not the other way around.**

Micro Reaccumulation Within a 5th Wave Setup

They are:

- Controlled by market makers / architects

- Designed to shake out impatient buyers

- A way to rebuild momentum after Wave 4 before the 5th wave launches

---

What They Represent Technically

1. Liquidity Collection & Testing:

- The 1-min 21 EMA becomes a grindline.

- Price dips below it? That's a liquidity test to trap late shorts.

- Bounces above? Buyers stepping in with precision — and often stealth volume.

2. RSI & DMI Confirm Structure:

During these micro waves:

- RSI is typically riding just above the base MA (bullish bias but suppressed).

- +DI starts rising, but not aggressively.

- ADX is either flat or starting to curl up — a major pre-breakout sign.

If you're seeing green delta candles during red prints, you're looking at hidden buyer footprints.

How to Read This:

These 1-min wavelets on the 21 EMA during sideways 5-min behavior are like heartbeat rhythms of accumulation. They're the final breaths before a sprint.

You're watching the "Coil Reload Phase":

- The real run hasn't begun, but the base is forming.
- Market makers are loading inventory without causing breakout volume — until it's time.

When It Turns Into the 5th Wave

Watch for:

- RSI on 5-min and 1-min breaking above base MA together

- +DI crossing over ADX on 5-min (after previously being under)

- Delta volume flipping aggressively green on a red candle

- A 5-min candle that touches or bounces off the 15-min 9 EMA

That's your greenlight if all 3 Time-Frames align and the structure on the 5-min is intact witht he 9 EMA above the 21 EMA..

Summary

What You're Seeing	What It Means
1-min waves on 21 EMA	Micro reaccumulation / coil reload
5-min trending flat on 21 EMA	Energy stack is preparing for ignition
15-min price near 9 EMA	Anchor support for Wave 5 setup
RSI/base MA rising slowly	Momentum building
Delta shows green on red	Hidden accumulation by smart money

Chapter 4: Coils and Compression Patterns

What is a Compression Coil Entry?

Imagine a spring getting squeezed tighter and tighter...
At some point, it *has* to release that built-up energy — violently — in one direction.

In trading, a **compression coil** is when:

- **Price volatility shrinks** (small candles, tight range).

- **Momentum indicators** (like RSI or MACD) flatten or slightly dip, but **don't collapse.**

- **Trend structure stays bullish** underneath.

It's the market **charging up** for the next big move **without breaking trend structure**.

Core Coil Mechanics
(Wave Mastery Model):

1. **RSI Dips Below the Base RSI MA**

   o This signals **cooling momentum** —
   like a "breathe in" phase before a
   wave push.

   o It gives price room to reset **without
   breaking structure**.

2. **RSI Curves Back Up and Reclaims the
   Base MA**

   o This is your *early signal* that
   momentum is recharging.

   o It's your **entry window** if structure
   and confluence hold.

3. **+DI Begins to Rise**

   o This means **buying pressure is
   building** again — not just candle
   color, but actual directional pressure.

4. **ADX Starts Rising**

   o ADX rising confirms **trend strength** is following the momentum.

   o It's the engine turning on behind the wave.

5. **-DI Begins to Fall or Flatten**

   o This is key: it tells you **sellers are backing off** — you're no longer fighting pressure.

So in Short:

The RSI shows you the wave tension. The DI lines show who's fighting. The ADX shows who's winning.

When all three confirm post-coil, you're not just entering off a guess — you're **catching the beginning of structured momentum.**

The Psychology Behind Coils

Why They Shake Out the Many and Load Up the Few

Coils are one of the most misunderstood — yet most powerful — patterns in trading.

To most retail traders, a coil appears like the momentum is fading, the energy is gone, and the price is "cooling off." They panic. They exit. Worse, they enter short.

But here's what's really happening:

The Great Misdirection

Coils are designed to disguise strength as weakness.

The candles begin to shrink.
Volume tapers off.
RSI slows or flattens.
ADX appears to fall.
And retail traders — trained to chase excitement — interpret this as a reversal or the end of the move.

But institutions think very differently.

What Institutions Are Really Doing

They are **reloading**.

Institutions need size — and size requires liquidity. If they buy too aggressively, they **move the market against themselves**. So instead, they manipulate:

- Small red candles with **positive delta**

- Reclaims of VWAP followed by micro dips

- RSI flattening just under the base MA

All of this keeps retail hesitant while they **quietly reload at better prices** — often just above the 21 EMA on the 1-minute chart.

They use **technical exhaustion** to **mask intention**.

The Short Seller's Trap

At the same time, short sellers see the move "stalling."

They spot:

- Lower highs

- Small red candles

- RSI rolling over

And they get bold.

But what they don't see is that **ADX has only dipped on the 1-minute**, not on the 5-minute or 15-minute. RSI may be coiling, but the base MA is **still rising**. VWAP is intact. Delta is green on red.

And when the institutions finish building their position...

> The coil breaks.

> Volume explodes.

> Shorts scramble to cover — creating the ignition fuel for Wave 3.

Your Edge: Don't React — Observe

For most traders, the appearance of a coil—those tight, slow candles moving sideways—signals uncertainty. To the untrained eye, the coil appears to be the market losing steam, a run that has exhausted itself. The energy seems gone, the volume slows, and price refuses to climb. This is when retail traders begin to panic. Their strategy, often reliant on momentum and emotion, fails to interpret what is happening beneath the surface.

But you are not the average trader.

Where most see hesitation, you see preparation. Where others see weakness, you see intent. The coil, in truth, is not a stall—it is the buildup. It is structure forming silently beneath the noise. It is the intentional compression of price, guided not by randomness but by design. The institutions are not absent here—they are active. They are reloading positions, collecting liquidity at controlled levels without moving price dramatically. This is the blueprint of the next expansion wave.

If you've prepared properly—if you've tracked the alignment of RSI base moving averages across multiple timeframes, monitored ADX for momentum health, and confirmed delta behavior inside the red candles—then the coil is not something to be feared. It is something to be welcomed.

This is where my edge comes into play.

You are no longer reacting to what price appears to be doing. You are observing what structure is telling you. You've developed a method of confirming accumulation before it becomes obvious, and that transforms the coil from a source of stress into a moment of opportunity. It becomes a test not just of your technical insight, but of your discipline.

The majority of traders still chase green candles and sell into red ones. But you now recognize that true opportunity does not announce itself with loud, bullish momentum. Instead, it forms quietly, in silence, beneath consolidation, and within the shadows of hesitation.

To trade the coil is to trade the structure. And structure is the only truth the market can't lie about.

When others exit early or misread the pullback, you remain still—not out of stubbornness, but out of understanding. You know what the indicators are whispering. You recognize the subtle rise of base RSI. You see that ADX is stabilizing before it accelerates again. You identify the delta activity that tells you buyers are still present, even as price momentarily dips.

You are no longer trading emotion. You are executing logic.

And that is the edge I've built. Quiet, refined, and patient.

This is not a strategy built on prediction—it's one built on observation. You wait for the structure to reveal itself. You watch as the market sets the trap for those who don't understand its language. And when your system confirms, you execute—not in fear, not in haste—but with certainty.

The coil is not your enemy. It is your invitation.

And only those who understand it can answer it.

The coil however can also be a double edged sword and stability can be used against you. When you see a coil forming and the initial breakout candle, keep in mind to look at the 1-Min ADX and if its been rising the last few minutes with the build up as well as if this candle is within the range of the 15-Min top Bollinger band. Institutions understand the dynamics of retail emotion and can often form a "fake" coil or break out to lure in buyers prior to the real move which is a liquidity sweep before the expansion run up.

Three Types of Coils

1. Stacked Coil

■ **Strongest** — institutional signature

- **Structure**: EMAs (usually 9 & 21) tightly stacked and flat

- **Price**: Compresses within a tight band, rarely breaking down

- **RSI**: Dips below base RSI MA, then reclaims it

- **+DI / ADX**: Gradually rise during the coil

- **Delta**: Often hidden buying or positive delta on red candles

- **Volume**: Low during coil, sharp spike on breakout

Entry: On reclaim of RSI base MA and first high-volume candle close
Why it works: It's engineered accumulation. Designed for release.

2. Sloped Coil

▲ **Moderate strength** — bullish but not aggressive

- **Structure**: 9 EMA angles downward slightly toward 21 EMA

- **Price**: Pulls back in steps, with candles leaning against 21 EMA

- **RSI**: Slower curl up, may lag the base

- **+DI / ADX**: Flat or gently rising

- **Volume**: Tapers off — reaccumulation phase, not active buildup

Entry: On reclaim of 9 EMA or RSI cross over base with positive delta
Why it works: Still bullish, but needs patience — often part of wave 2 or pre-5th wave reload

---

3. Curved Coil

▲ **Lowest probability** — potential fakeout setup

- **Structure**: EMAs begin to curve downward or lose slope integrity

- **Price**: Looks like a base but *drifts* without firm reclaim

- **RSI**: Below base RSI MA, may cross up weakly

- **+DI / ADX**: Both fading or weak

- **Delta**: Often neutral or "dead volume"

- **Volume**: Flat — no build, no commitment

Entry: Avoid until proven — needs strong reclaim candle *with* volume
Why it often fails: Coils form without buyers behind them — it's resting, not building

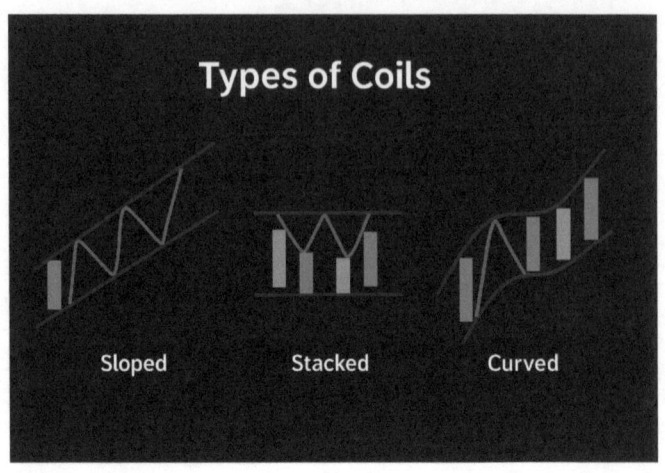

Key Signs of a Compression Coil Summary

Category	What You See	Meaning
Price	Tight candles, sideways chop, small bodies	Market is consolidating energy
VWAP / EMA	Price hovers near or slightly dips into VWAP/short EMAs (like 9 EMA, 21 EMA)	No real breakdown — just a reset

Bollinger Bands	Bands start to **narrow** after expansion	Volatility compression = pressure cooker
Volume	Volume **dries up** during coil phase	No real selling pressure, just lack of buyers momentarily
RSI	Dips or flattens near the base but **stays positive**	Momentum reset without trend breaking
DI+/ADX (Directional Movement)	+DI still dominant or ADX slowly rising	Overall trend strength is still building

The Psychology Behind It

- Retail traders **panic** because of the slowdown.

- Institutions **reload** at better prices without moving the market.

- Short sellers **pile in** during the micro-dip, thinking it's over — **only to get trapped** when price explodes upward.

It's an intentional shakeout to **build fuel** for the next **wave up**

1. **Expansion Move**
   Big green candles (Opening morning high with a gap up and big green candles on the lower time frames).

2. **First Pullback**
   RSI pulls back (on lower timeframe like 1-min), price holds VWAP/9 EMA.

3. **Coil Phase**
   Price goes sideways, low volume, candles shrink, Bollinger Bands start to pinch.

4. **Micro Signals Inside Coil**

   • 1-Min RSI returns to base and turns slightly up.

   • Tiny bullish hammers form on 1-min.

   • Slight uptick in volume.

5. **Explosion**
   A sudden huge candle rips through the coil top, squeezing shorts and forcing buyers to FOMO.

Checklist to Confirm a Compression Coil Entry

◼ RSI dips but doesn't fully collapse (baselining).
◼ Price hovers around VWAP or 9/21 EMA (no breakdown).
◼ Bollinger Bands compress.
◼ +DI on higher timeframe still winning.
◼ Volume dries up on pullback candles.
◼ No major bearish structure breaks on 5-min / 15-min.

Why It's SO Powerful

- **Lowest risk entries** — because you're buying tight against support (VWAP/EMA).

- **Biggest reward** — because you catch the explosive move from the very first candle.

- **Psychologically strong** — you're NOT chasing high green candles. You're buying when others are scared/confused.

How Elite Traders Use It

Elite scalpers and swing traders **wait** for these setups instead of chasing momentum blindly.
 They *specialize* in spotting these compression coils after big expansions — it's like buying a "ticket to the next wave" at a discount.

Quick Summary

- Coil = **energy reset**, not trend break.

- Watch RSI baselining.

- Watch Bollinger squeeze.

- Confirm trend strength.

- Enter near VWAP or EMA during the tight chop.

⊚ Level 1: Soft Coil (The "Easy" One)

What it looks like:

- Very obvious pullback into VWAP or 9 EMA.

- Bollinger Bands narrow slightly.

- Price gently drifts sideways — NO major dips.

- RSI dips just a little but holds well above 50.

- Volume shrinks in a "calm" way.

Psychology:
This is when *everyone* knows it's a healthy pullback. Very beginner-friendly. Lots of "buy-the-dip" crowd.

Power of the move:
■ Good, but not insane.
■ ~5-10% move usually.

⑥ Level 2: Medium Coil (The "Trap Setup")

What it looks like:

- Price actually *dips* a little deeper — sometimes briefly under VWAP or 9 EMA.

- Bollinger Bands pinch much tighter.

- RSI dips closer to base (~45–50 zone).

- You might see a quick fake breakdown candle.

- Volume *shrinks hard* — almost "dead air" for a few candles.

Psychology:
This one **fakes out weak longs**. Retail traders panic and sell too early.
Smart money reloads here while shorts get confident.

Power of the move:
■ Much bigger — 10-20% move if setup resolves upward.

⑥ Level 3: Hard Coil (The "Monster Trap")

What it looks like:

- Price looks like it's **breaking down**: wicks under key supports (VWAP/EMA) but closes *right back inside*.

- Bollinger Bands are *super tight*, almost a "straight line."

- RSI almost kisses 40 or even 35 — then sharply snaps back up.

- Big scary-looking red candles with **no follow through**.

- Micro sweeps (sweep lows under structure) happen.

- +DI stays strong on higher timeframes (5-min, 15-min) — hidden strength.

Psychology:
Maximum fear. Retail traders *sell* into the low.
Short sellers *add shorts aggressively*.
Institutions **trap everyone** — then nuke them when the coil explodes upward.

Power of the move:

■ ✹ Insane — 20-40% rip sometimes within 15-30 minutes.

■ **Quick Visual Table**

Type	Look	Emotion It Creates	Power of Breakout
Soft Coil	Gentle drift sideways	Calm "dip buyers"	Good (5-10%)
Medium Coil	Deeper dip + tiny fakeouts	Doubt + minor fear	Strong (10-20%)
Hard Coil	Violent wick under support + trap	Panic + short confidenc e	Massive (20-40%)

Which One Should You Hunt For?

Medium Coil and Hard Coil are goldmines for this style.

Because:

- You're trading strong runners already.

- You're timing reload entries **after** an emotional flush.

- You want *fast explosive pops* — not slow grinds.

Your Trading Checklist

Checklist	Confirmed?
Bollinger Bands squeezing tight	■
RSI pulling back but baselining	■
VWAP or 9 EMA holding price structure	■
Volume drying up during chop	■
Higher timeframes (+DI > ADX) still bullish	■
Micro sweeps or fakeouts complete	■
1-min RSI turning upward off the base	■

Chapter 5: Fakeouts and How to Avoid Them

Common Fakeout Signals

- RSI spikes above 70 but quickly falls back below 60 within 3 candles.
- Bollinger Band expansion without volume.
- 1-min coil breakouts not aligning with 5-min trend.
- +DI begins falling while ADX flattens on the higher time frames.
- Price on the lower timeframe trends up while **ADX falls** and RSI MA base flattens or rises but is followed by rejection on the next candle (This one has caught me off guard a few times when hyper focusing on the set up)

Fakeout Filters

- Use RSI MA base on the 1-min: failure for the rsi to reach it during a coil = low conviction, allow it to cross over and pull back to verify support. The RSI Base MA should continue to rise as the RSI pulls back to reload on the micro level; for the 3rd wave this would mean the coil is forming on the 1-Min chart.
- Require rising ADX on both 5-min and 15-min before considering an entry. Needless to say during the wave 2 pull back

after a morning gap up the 1-Min ADX will have retraced down along with the RSI BASE MA during the coil build up. However the ADX on the 1-Min should reverse up for at least 2-3 candles prior to any expansion move to build up support otherwise I assume it's a trap and let the trade pass regardless.

- No entry without volume > 50k on the 5-min trigger candle or relative volume greater than 100% for the day within the early morning session. The greater the relative volume the better. It's not uncommon for me to trade tickers with volume in excess of 200x or more showing institutional presence.

- If a stock is rising after pullback along the 5 min 21 EMA and the RSI is rising along with the structure but the Base RSI MA has not reversed, you're looking at distribution not accumulation.

Avoiding Traps in Downtrends During Wave Plays

In intraday wave setups, structural alignment between price action and moving averages is everything. Many failed trades stem not from poor strategy, but from forcing a setup into the wrong market context.

When attempting to play the wave structure—especially third or fifth wave entries—avoid taking trades on downtrending stocks, even if the RSI and ADX begin to reverse upward. A major red flag is when the 9 EMA stays below the 21 EMA on the 5-minute chart for an extended period. This is a strong indication of a weakening trend structure and fading liquidity.

This is particularly risky if the third wave fails and the stock has been trending down for over an hour. It may look like it's curling back up, but in reality, the energy has already dissipated.

It's acceptable for the 9 EMA to temporarily fall back and retest or "butt up" against the 21 EMA. However, the 21 EMA should continue to trend upward and must not decisively flatten or roll over. A quick recovery in the 21 EMA reinforces the uptrend and confirms that buyers are still in control.

This structure matters because it allows for liquidity to flow cleanly—enabling the stock to move from the 9 EMA on the third wave to the 21 EMA on the fifth wave. If the EMAs lose alignment, that liquidity bridge disappears, and price action becomes choppy, manipulated, and unreliable.

💡 **Micro-tip:** If the 9 EMA touches the 21 EMA but there's no immediate bounce with increasing volume, skip the trade. It likely won't recover fast enough for a clean wave structure.

⚠️ **Mindset Warning:** Don't let hope override structure. Just because indicators flash green doesn't mean the setup is valid. Downtrends are deceptive—"structure comes first, confirmation second, emotion never."

When ADX Reverses Up Before the Base RSI MA

It *looks* like strength, but it's
misleading if RSI isn't confirming yet.

This is a **trap condition** — a disguised *divergence of intent*.

▲ Why It Happens:

- **ADX** measures **trend strength**, but **not direction**.

- So a rising ADX just means **momentum is increasing**, regardless of whether it's bullish or bearish.

- **If RSI's base MA is still sloping down or flat**, the buyers aren't fully committed — *yet*.

- That's when **"architects" push a fake breakout**, triggering FOMO — just to **exit into it**.

▼ What It Means:

- **The coil is premature.**

- **The breakout is a sweep.**

- **Volume may spike,** but **RSI isn't confirming sustainable direction.**

- You'll often see a **strong candle,** a wick above premarket levels, and then — a rug pull.

■ **True Confirmation Checklist Before Entry:**

To avoid that exact trap:

1. **RSI crosses above its base MA** *before* or *with* the ADX reversal.

2. **+DI** is rising and separating from **-DI.**

3. **Volume delta** on the red candle is positive (buying under red).

4. **1-min coil** is forming with volume build, not release.

5. **Candle closes near the high**, not with a long upper wick.

6. **The 5-min RSI base is rising** at the same time as ADX — this means alignment.

Mindset Shift:

If ADX leads *without RSI confirmation*, you're watching **a narrative** — not a structure.

It's the **illusion of strength**.
That's how market makers disguise distribution as breakout.

"The market doesn't pay you for potential. It pays you for precision."

"If the wave wants to run, it'll come back for you. Let the structure align — not your emotions."

"Reading the Intention Before the Confirmation"

How Delta and RSI Signal the Pressure Before It Moves the Candle

> A pullback isn't weakness.
> It's a breath.
>
> With rising RSI, a strong ADX,
> and a fake red candle
> holding green delta, it's
> not a sell signal —
> it's a **coil reload.**
>
> "The red candle is the setup.
> The delta is the tell."

Delta + RSI as Leading Indicators (vs. DMI as a Result)

You're now using delta and RSI as leading indicators — tools that help you sense where the pressure is building before the chart reacts.

Here's the breakdown:

■ Delta (Order Flow Insight)
Shows intentional buying or selling before it's confirmed on the candle

When paired with a red candle + positive delta, it's a sign of absorption or buyers hiding beneath weakness

Especially powerful during coils, reload zones, or EMA pressure points

Delta isn't always perfect for direction, but it's often perfect for timing
Delta doesn't dictate direction. Structure does.

Delta shows pressure. Structure shows permission.

When those align — you're in the game.
When they diverge — you're just watching the final breath before the sweep.

■ RSI + Base MA
When RSI rises off the base MA with strength and angle, you're seeing momentum reload

If it stalls or flattens while price is holding above an EMA, it often signals coiling before a push

Think of RSI as the energy curve — the tide rolling up toward the wave

✘ DMI / +DI / ADX (Result Indicators)

These confirm what already happened — they validate structure

A strong ADX confirms a move is healthy and can run further which is why as a lagging indicator its always important to note it should have reversed up prior.

But as you've likely seen, ADX often lags the entry window and +DI/-DI can whipsaw meaning if you;ve noticed the coil forming and DMI building strength you'll take a position prior to expansion.

Best used for:

Confirming that the direction you're seeing in Delta/RSI is supported

Avoiding fakeouts or weak trends

Grading your setup's strength, not identifying the entry

You're no longer just stacking indicators — you're building hierarchies:

Delta says: pressure's coming
RSI says: momentum is shifting
Structure says: here's where we are in the wave
DMI says: now it's real

"I don't hunt the market. I listen for alignment. Structure shows me the stage, confluence confirms the actors, and delta whispers when the scene is about to shift."

Sometimes the wave doesn't warn you. It tests you. It fakes the fall, sweeps the floor, and then shows you who's still in the room.

When delta is quiet, structure speaks louder. When the 21 EMA is violated with a deep wick and instant reclaim, watch for the RSI crossover and rising ADX — that's when the wave isn't coming… it's already started.

Why 5-Min Delta is often Stronger Than 1-Min Delta

	1-Min Delta	5-Min Delta
Reactivity	Fast signal	Slower, but more solid
Whipsaw risk	Higher	Lower
Noise	More	Filtered
Confidence in structure	Weaker	Stronger
Entry timing	Sharper	Sometimes late (but confirms the play is real)

Psychology Behind the Setup:

Market makers allow the candle to close red to invite short pressure
Meanwhile, buyers are quietly stepping in — evidenced by the positive delta
Price is held down, but volume tells a different story
The next candle typically ignites upward, confirming the absorption and starting the real wave

Why It Works:

Most traders react to candles. This setup teaches you to listen to volume.

The Red Delta Coil is a signal from the smart money. When you learn to read the story behind the wick, you stop chasing the wave — and start entering just before it lifts.

1 & 5 Min Positive Delta Chart

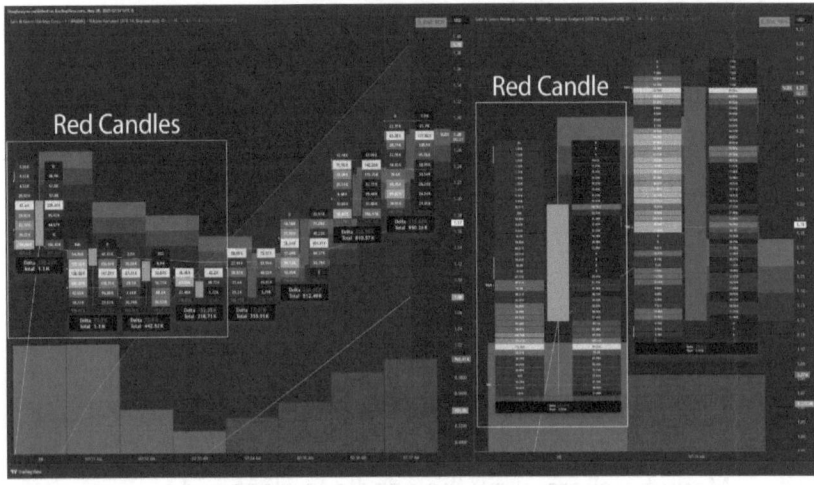

Red candles forming during the coil, yet printing positive delta, signal quiet buyer demand building beneath the surface — a subtle but powerful clue that a breakout run is approaching.

Disguised Distribution: When the Market Appears Strong, But Isn't

In the realm of intraday wave trading, one of the most deceptive and costly traps for retail traders is *Phase 4 Distribution disguised as strength.* The setup often looks bullish on the surface — a reclaimed VWAP, structure intact, and slowly rising candles — but beneath it all, the engine has stalled. When a stock's external strength masks internal weakness, you're witnessing the artistry of institutional offloading.

The Setup: A Market That "Should" Run

You'll often see:

- **VWAP reclaimed**, signaling renewed buying interest.

- **Structure holding** — no break below the 1-minute or 5-minute 21 EMA.

- **RSI goes sideways**, and **ADX begins a quiet decline**.

- Meanwhile, **Delta stays positive**, even as red candles stack.

This confluence of events *looks* like strength, but it is, in truth, the beginning of the end for that move.

The stock may still grind higher — slowly, mechanically — but the fuel that carried it upward is fading. And if you're paying attention to the internals, you'll sense it.

Why This Happens: The Hidden Mechanics

This isn't classic accumulation. It's a *stealth distribution* — the phase when institutions are no longer building positions but *unloading* into the hands of unaware buyers.

- **RSI Going Sideways**
  When RSI stops rising, it's telling you that **buying pressure has stalled**. There is no new demand — just the residue of momentum. Price may continue rising for a few candles, but it's coasting, not climbing.

- **ADX Declining While Price Rises**
  A falling ADX during a rising price is the *ultimate divergence*. Institutions are easing their participation. It's not about panic-selling — it's about *tactically distributing* shares into perceived strength while momentum quietly evaporates.

- **Positive Delta on Red Candles**
  This is the final mask. Retail sees red candles and assumes weakness, but the delta tells the real story: **aggressive buying into weakness**. The institutions are

creating liquidity — and then using it to exit.

Accumulation vs Distribution — Know the Difference

Behavior	Accumulation	Distribution
RSI	Rising with base MA	Sideways or lagging
ADX	Rising or curving up	Falling even as price rises
Delta	Green on red candles (with strength)	Green on red candles (with fading ADX)
Structure	Forms off the 21 EMA coil	Micro-pullbacks build false structure
VWAP	Built beneath as a base	Reclaimed, then used to trap

ADX: The Institutional Brake Pedal

Institutions don't rely on RSI or price alone — they move with conviction and manage risk via momentum. **ADX is the tell.**

- When it rises, they're pressing the gas.

- When it flattens or falls — despite rising price — they're *tapping the brakes* and exiting.
  If **RSI is stalling** and **ADX is dropping**, the green candles are just a sleight of hand. Retail is holding the bag.

Why Day Delta is Often Hidden

Cumulative delta, especially over a session, exposes too much. It reveals accumulation, distribution, and imbalance. Many platforms obscure it intentionally or by design, making it difficult for retail traders to follow the footprint of the architects. By layering red candles and spreading volume thin, institutions maintain *stealth* — but not invisibility.

Chapter 6: Backtesting Strategy

Backtest Criteria

1. Use replay mode on TradingView.
2. Begin with 15-min chart and identify strong bullish or bearish trends.
3. Zoom into 5-min and 1-min to locate coil or retracement to EMA zones.
4. Record setups only if RSI, ADX, and volume align.

Logging Entries

- Use a spreadsheet to log: Entry Time, Ticker, Setup Type (Wave 3 or 5), RSI/ADX Levels, EMA Alignment, Volume.
- Add notes on coil shape and fakeout risk.
- Review outcome after 10, 30, and 60 minutes.

Statistics to Track

- Win rate by wave type.
- Average % move after entry.
- Stopout reasons (EMA violation, ADX drop, etc.).

Chapter 7: Architects and Builders – The Market's Hidden Engineers

Every run you chase, every pullback you study, and every breakout you aim to ride has a blueprint—one not always visible at first glance. Behind the surface of candlesticks and indicators lies a deeper layer of influence: the market architects and builders.

Who Are the Architects and Builders?

In wave theory trading, the architects are the institutional players—market makers, hedge funds, and algorithmic forces—that initiate and design the larger wave structures. They lay the foundation for the movement. Builders are the liquidity providers, retail momentum followers, and volume clusters that help the structure take shape. Together, they engineer the phases of a stock's run.

Think of it this way:

Architects design the macro structure—the higher time frame (15-min, 30-min, 1-hour) movement where the big money sets up its trap.

Builders execute the microstructure—the 1-min and 5-min movements that create the illusion of randomness but actually serve as the framework for engineered runs.

The Flow of Waves: A Constructed Sequence

The market does not run impulsively without preparation. Smart money accumulates before a run and distributes into strength. Understanding this is key to decoding wave formations.

Wave 1 (The Blueprint Reveal)

Often initiated with a sudden increase in volume or volatility.

Usually shallow and uncertain, built to test interest and trap early chasers.

Architect's goal: Reveal intent without disclosing full blueprint.

Wave 2 (The Pullback & Trap)

The pullback creates a buying opportunity at the EMA—usually the 9 EMA on 5-min.

Most traders perceive this as a rejection, but builders quietly step in to reload.

Liquidity is absorbed at optimal prices.

RSI may dip, but the +DI remains elevated or consolidates.

Wave 3 (The Structural Release)

The explosive move designed to draw in retail traders.

Builders ride the volume surge, while architects may start distributing slowly into strength.

This is where your strategy shines: indicators are in alignment, and momentum is visible across timeframes.

The energy stack is fully charged—EMAs converge, RSI is elevated, ADX rises.

Wave 4 (Distribution Coil)

The "pause" in the run.

Coils form here to mask distribution or prepare for a 5th wave push.

This is also where fakeouts and shakeouts are engineered.

Architect's move: Exhaust retail optimism and rebalance sentiment.

Wave 5 (Final Push or Trap Wave)

May mimic wave 3 but often lacks the same volume conviction.

If volume is present and RSI stays strong, it can be a valid entry.

Builders load early, driving a smaller but fast move.

If RSI or ADX fail to confirm, this becomes the final trap before reversal.

Design Principles of Market Engineers

To the average trader, the price chart is a battlefield of noise—conflicting signals, chaotic candles, and unpredictable movement. But to the market engineer—to the architect behind the wave—every move is deliberate, each structure crafted with intention. These are not random fluctuations. They are blueprints in motion, and behind them are builders—institutions—designing liquidity traps, exits, entries, and expansions with calculated precision.

Liquidity zones are not just reaction points. They are construction sites. In these zones, market architects gather the volume needed to enter or exit large positions without tipping the scales. And the coils that form there? They are not accidental—they are engineered. Tight consolidation patterns, false breakdowns, abrupt wicks to key EMAs, and the sudden appearance of news-driven candles—these are all structural components. Like scaffolding around a skyscraper, they mask the true purpose beneath: to prepare for a move that will only become obvious after it's too late to catch.

Volume becomes the fuel for this design. No builder starts the engine without a full tank, and in trading, that fuel is liquidity. Each wave is not just a result of buyers or sellers—it's a mechanism designed to trigger stops, provoke shorts into position, or entice retail buyers to chase. Spikes in volume during these moments are not anomalies. They are deliberate injections of energy. A shakeout candle isn't simply volatility—it's fuel consumption before takeoff.

The alignment of key moving averages acts as the framework. Institutions rely heavily on the 5-minute 9 EMA and the centerline of the 15-minute Bollinger Band to shape the core of the move. These are not arbitrary indicators—they're structural anchors. When the 1-minute 21 EMA aligns with either of these higher timeframe markers, it's a sign that the builders have chosen their path. This alignment often triggers high-frequency trading algorithms, which launch the price through resistance or defend key zones in milliseconds. To the naked eye, the move seems fast. But to the engineer, it was just the next step in the plan.

RSI and ADX are the pulse and pressure gauge of this structure. RSI doesn't just measure strength—it tells you whether the market is diverging from its prior path or reverting to equilibrium. Divergence often marks exhaustion, but reversion is the heartbeat of an uptrend. Meanwhile, ADX does not care about direction. It is the metric of intensity. When ADX rises and +DI gains dominance, it's a signal that the foundation of the move is solid. **The builders will not accelerate until this integrity is confirmed so keep this in mind.**

This is how you read the blueprint in real time.

It's not about chasing the move. It's about understanding the engineering behind it—recognizing that each fakeout is a tool, each pullback a measurement, and each spike in volume a calculated pour of concrete into a foundation that was drawn long before the breakout began.

To trade like a professional, you must stop reacting to what the market is doing and start interpreting what it's building.

Reading the Build Before the Breakout

To truly trade like a professional, you must develop the skill to see what the architects are constructing—long before the general public realizes what's happening. The institutions do not leave obvious clues. They build beneath the surface, beneath the noise, and often beneath the very indicators most retail traders rely on. But for those who understand how to interpret structure, the signs are clear, even if subtle.

The first of these signs is the presence of an accumulation coil—those compact, disciplined zones of sideways movement you'll find on the 1-minute and 5-minute charts. These are not random pauses. They are the trenches. The hidden foundation of the move. It is here that large buyers or sellers accumulate or offload shares without disrupting the broader market. The tighter and more controlled the coil, the more deliberate the design. This is not consolidation; it is construction.

From here, volume becomes a language. Look for the small but intentional spikes—volume bursts without significant price movement. These are tests. Builders probing the market, checking how much supply remains, how easily price can be moved, and how traders are positioned. These tests are often overlooked, but they reveal intent. If price doesn't move but volume ticks upward, the market isn't undecided—it's being measured.

Multi-timeframe RSI adds the next layer of structure validation. If RSI is compressing high on the 15-minute and 30-minute charts—hovering in elevated zones but refusing to fall—then the structure is still being reinforced. The building is not complete. The market is not yet ready for release. This RSI behavior, when aligned across timeframes, shows the tightening spring beneath the surface.

But for every structure built, there comes a point of exhaustion. And just as buildings rise, they must also fall. The very architects who constructed the wave, who accumulated in silence and released the move with precision, are also the ones who dismantle it—either by reversing direction or by liquidating their positions into the euphoria of late buyers. If you ignore the signs, you will become the exit liquidity.

So how do you protect yourself from this demolition phase?

The first warning is in the RSI. As momentum fades, RSI will begin to slope downward—not just on the 1-minute chart but across all key timeframes. What was once an aligned multi-timeframe compression will begin to break. You may even see short-term RSI rise while higher timeframe RSI flattens or falls. That is a signal of internal weakness and distribution.

Next, you must observe the relationship between +DI and ADX. When these two no longer support the move—when +DI begins to decline while ADX peaks or flattens—it suggests the engine is losing power. Momentum without confirmation is noise.

Then come the EMAs. When price begins to close below key EMAs across multiple timeframes—especially the 1-minute 21 EMA, the 5-minute 9 EMA, and the 15-minute Bollinger Band to to centerline—the foundation begins to crack. And the final tell? Volume vanishes. The breakout attempts lose power. There are no builders left—only those late to the party.

This is not the time to be brave.

This is the time to step aside. Exit the structure before it collapses. The move has already happened. The profits have already been made. The blueprint is complete.

And now, your job is simple: scout the next build. Start from the trenches again. Because the market always builds another wave. The professionals aren't chasing breakouts—they're tracking blueprints.

Final Thoughts

Understanding that the market is not random, but deliberately engineered, changes how you trade. You're no longer reacting—you're reading blueprints. The better you get at identifying the architects' intentions and the builders' confirmations, the more consistent and confident your entries will become.

This chapter serves as a reminder: you're not just trading candles. You're navigating structures—some meant to support you, others meant to trap you. Learn the language of design, and you'll always be a step ahead.

Chapter 8: Psychological Blueprints – How Market Architects Bait the Masses

Understanding price action is not enough. To truly evolve as a trader, you must decode *intent*—the emotional traps built into the structure of every engineered move. This chapter pulls back the curtain on how market architects manipulate mass psychology to orchestrate liquidity events, bait retail traders, and execute high-probability trades.

Engineered Emotion: The Fuel Behind Institutional Strategy

Professional traders do not merely react to price—they design the market environment itself. Behind every sudden breakout, sharp pullback, or dramatic reversal is often a deliberate intent: to provoke emotion.

These engineered patterns are not about randomness or chaos. They are carefully constructed to inspire specific behavioral responses from retail traders. When you see a sudden surge in price, what you're often witnessing is not organic demand, but a spark designed to ignite fear of missing out. It's a move meant to attract breakout chasers—those who enter impulsively, convinced a major run is beginning. And once they're in, their liquidity becomes part of the structure.

Equally calculated are the sharp drops. These aren't always market corrections. Many are controlled demolitions—meant to trigger stop-losses, induce panic-selling, and shake out those who bought early. The resulting volume provides the perfect cover for institutions to accumulate quietly while retail traders exit in fear.

False confidence is another weapon. The market might rally just enough to appear healthy, only to stall at a key resistance or EMA level. Retail traders, feeling reassured, may double down—believing the move is genuine. But behind the scenes, professionals are fading the move, offloading positions while others build them.

Why does this happen?

Because emotion creates volume—and volume is liquidity.

Institutional players cannot simply enter or exit massive positions without impacting price. If they tried to buy or sell outright, the market would react too quickly, reducing their edge. Instead, they rely on retail emotion to provide the liquidity they need. Every surge of greed or wave of fear becomes an opportunity to place or offload large orders without drawing attention.

This is the hidden game.

What feels like momentum to most traders is often a mirage—a cleverly constructed sequence to draw in volume. The real move happens after the trap is set. The real structure reveals itself only to those who see beneath the surface.

To succeed at this level, you must detach from emotion and begin to observe the purpose behind price. Ask yourself: *Why now? Who benefits?*

Once you understand that emotion is engineered, you stop becoming its victim. You stop reacting—and begin positioning yourself like an architect, not an audience.

1. The Illusion of Momentum

What you see: A strong green candle breaks out of a coil with high volume.

What's happening: The architects have already loaded and are now drawing in retail buyers to sell into.

Emotional trigger: "It's going to explode. I can't miss this one."

2. The "Support" Setup

What you see: A textbook bounce off VWAP or EMA.

What's happening: A bait candle is built, often closing high, only to reverse and slam through support.

Emotional trigger: "This is the bounce I was waiting for. I'm buying the dip."

3. The Reversal Fakeout

What you see: Hammer candle forms after a falling knife. RSI is low.

What's happening: Builders initiate a false reversal setup to absorb liquidity.

Emotional trigger: "That was the bottom—it's reversing now."

4. The Extended Run Stretch

What you see: Price has already moved 30%, but keeps ticking up in small candles.

What's happening: Institutions are distributing slowly into thinning volume.

Emotional trigger: "It's still going—I'm going to ride the last leg."

Emotional Phases Within a Wave

Each wave of price movement has emotional fingerprints. Here's how emotions evolve in a 5-wave run:

Wave 1 – Curiosity & Skepticism

"Is this really moving? Probably just a fake pump."

Wave 2 – Relief & Regret

"It's pulling back. I knew it wasn't real... wait, I should've entered."

Wave 3 – Euphoria & Chase Mode

"I don't want to miss this! I'm in now, it's going to the moon!"

Wave 4 – Doubt & Confusion

"Is it done? Should I sell? What if it bounces again?"

Wave 5 – Greed & Panic Exit

"One more push! Wait—it's reversing. Get out, get out!"

Institutions study this psychological rhythm like a metronome. They trigger it deliberately to harvest liquidity.

How to Flip the Script

"The winning trader isn't the one who sees the pattern first—they're the one who understands why it exists."

Here's how to mentally stay ahead:

1. View setups as traps first. Ask: "If I were trying to bait others, would I build this?

2. Use indicators for confirmation, not comfort.RSI, ADX, and volume should support the intent, not just the shape.

3. Never chase a candle—chase confluence. When price, volume, EMAs, RSI, and time-of-day align, the psychology is real—not fabricated.

4. Recognize fake strength. True strength builds on rising volume and clean structure. If the volume is dry or jumpy, it's likely a trap.

This chapter isn't just about psychology—it's about survival. Every candle you trade is part of a larger narrative. If you don't know the story, you become the liquidity.

Market makers don't fear your technical skill—they bet on your emotional responses. And unless you understand the emotional architecture, even the best setup can turn into a loss.

But when you master this lens, everything changes. You'll start to see the real move building before it triggers. You'll wait patiently at the right zone. You'll act with confidence while others hesitate.

Closing Thought

The market is a game of manipulation disguised as movement. It's not the cleanest setup that wins—it's the one that understands both structure and psychology.

The Real Edge

Here's the truth most won't tell you:

The setup isn't your edge—your discipline is.

Anyone can spot a hammer candle.

Few will wait patiently for it to retest VWAP, print volume confirmation, and trap retail first.

That's where you separate from the crowd.

The Master Blueprint isn't a fixed script—it's a living system. You'll refine it over time as your pattern recognition sharpens and your emotional control strengthens to make it your own.

Final Thought

You didn't come this far to chase random trades. You came to master the structure behind the move—the blueprint that only true professionals see.

Now, you have it.
Use it wisely.

Chapter 9: The Trader Development Stages

From Chaser to Architect – The 5 Stages of Trader Evolution

Most traders focus on entries and exits. Professionals focus on identity. Where you are on the curve determines what you need to study—and what will destroy you if you skip ahead. This chapter helps you locate yourself, correct your blind spots, and step into mastery the right way.

Stage 1 – The Pattern Chaser

Mindset: "If I find the right setup, I'll win."

Behavior: Trades every breakout, no context. Lives on TikTok and Reddit setups.

Pain Point: Emotional overtrading, chasing green candles, no stop-loss discipline.

Goal: Learn to recognize structure before reaction.

■ Graduation Key: Learns that price action without context is noise.

Stage 2 – The Confirmation Seeker

Mindset: "I need proof before I enter."

Behavior: Waits for indicators to align, often enters too late.

Pain Point: Misses moves, loses confidence, overanalyzes.

Goal: Trust setup over emotion. See opportunity forming, not formed.

■ Graduation Key: Begins anticipating setups, not reacting to them.

Stage 3 – The System Builder

Mindset: "I need rules and structure."

Behavior: Builds a framework. Logs trades. Finds consistent entries.

Pain Point: Over-optimization, rigid expectations, data overwhelm.

Goal: Balance flexibility with discipline. Know when to adapt.

■ Graduation Key: Understands market context overrides fixed rules.

Stage 4 – The Tactical Strategist

Mindset: "The market speaks in structure and timeframes."

Behavior: Trades only top-tier setups. Uses multi-timeframe energy alignment.

Pain Point: Exit timing. Struggles between letting profits run or locking them in.

Goal: Refine confidence in scale-outs, trust the wave thesis.

■ Graduation Key: Learns to spot traps before the breakout even begins.

Stage 5 – The Architect

Mindset: "Price is the result of engineered emotion."

Behavior: Builds trades like puzzles. Waits in silence. Spots intent in structure.

Pain Point: None acute—just maintaining patience and humility.

Goal: Teach, evolve, and stay detached from ego.

■ Graduation Key: No longer trades to prove—trades to execute.

The Trader's Manifesto

The Market doesn't reward noise. It rewards precision.

I will trade when all timeframes align.

I will enter where the wolves eat—not where the rabbits run.

I will journal not just trades, but lessons.

I will ignore the crowd and honor my coil.

I will never chase green. I will plan for red.

I will respect time—because time structures the wave.

When others see panic, I see positioning.

When others chase emotion, I wait for alignment.

I am not here to gamble.

I am here to architect.

This is my edge. This is my craft. This is my wave.

🎥 See It in Motion: @HoodiesAndHunger on YouTube

If you've made it this far, then you already know: This isn't just a trading strategy. It's a way of seeing the market differently. It's structure first, confluence second, entry third — always.

But sometimes, even the clearest ideas hit harder when you **see them live.** That's why I created **@hoodiesandhunger** on YouTube.

This channel is where I break down everything from:

- Real-time trade examples

- Chart reviews of coils, structure, and delta

- My full pre-market process

- Trade recaps, breakdowns, and journal lessons

- Psychology, mistakes, and how I correct them

You'll see how I analyze entries off the 1-min 21 EMA, how I read RSI behavior **in waves**, and how I use positive delta on red candles as confirmation — all in real trades, not theory.

> This is the visual companion to the book — built for the traders who want to sharpen their eyes and tighten their edge.

Whether you're just starting or already refining your own system, this content is raw, honest, and actionable.

💬 **No fluff. No hype. Just structure, execution, and growth.**
📍 YouTube: **@hoodiesandhunger**
🎥 Come see what the market looks like through the eyes of a builder.

Conclusion

This wave-based strategy relies on discipline, alignment, and preparation. The 3rd wave offers explosive reward with the right structure, while the 5th wave gives redemption after consolidation. The key to consistent profitability lies in refusing subpar entries and only acting when all parameters align across timeframes.

This is a professional-grade strategy that, if followed methodically, sets the foundation for long-term trading success.

Charting & Platform Attribution

Some charts and examples in this book were generated using TradingView® (tradingview.com), a widely used platform for market charting and technical analysis. TradingView® is a registered trademark of TradingView Inc. This book is not affiliated with, endorsed by, or sponsored by TradingView Inc.

All charts included are the author's original screenshots created for personal use and educational demonstration. Any use of TradingView content is in accordance with fair use guidelines for educational purposes.

Glossary: Mastering Market Waves

ADX (Average Directional Index)

A trend strength indicator. In my system, rising ADX confirms structural integrity during wave setups. ADX doesn't show direction—only whether the market has strong momentum.

+DI / -DI (Directional Indicators)

Components of the ADX system. +DI shows bullish pressure, -DI bearish pressure. You look for +DI dominance with rising ADX as a green light for entries. If +DI falls below ADX, the setup is losing strength.

Architects

Institutional players—hedge funds, market makers, and algorithms—who engineer macro price movements. They build the higher timeframe structures and psychological traps.

Builders

Retail momentum traders and liquidity providers who fill out the architects' plans. Builders contribute to the energy stack and help fuel wave progression, especially on lower timeframes.

Bollinger Bands

Volatility-based bands used to spot compression and expansion. A narrowing Bollinger Band often signals an upcoming explosive move when aligned with coil structure and RSI baselining.

Coil

A compression pattern signaling a pause in price before an explosive continuation. Can be flat, sloped, or stacked. The tighter the coil, the stronger the release. The core concept behind "energy stacking."

Compression Coil Entry

A textbook entry strategy where price consolidates tightly against key EMAs or VWAP, indicating pent-up energy. Entry comes on the volume break with full alignment of trend strength.

EMA (Exponential Moving Average)

Key dynamic support/resistance tools. I rely on the 9 EMA, 21 EMA, and their alignment across timeframes (1-min, 5-min, 15-min, 30-min) to confirm structure. Entry often happens at EMA touches or overlaps.

Energy Stack

The synchronized alignment of all core indicators—EMAs, RSI, ADX, +DI/-DI, and volume—in a single direction. When the energy stack is clean, a move is imminent and high-probability.

Fakeout

A deceptive move designed to trap traders. Common fakeout signs in my system include RSI spikes with no follow-through, volume breaks without alignment, or misaligned coil breakouts.

FOMO (Fear of Missing Out)

A psychological trigger used by market architects to bait emotional retail entries. In my framework, successful traders wait *through* FOMO zones, not chase them.

Hammer Candle

A bullish reversal candle with a long lower wick. Used in my entries during coil reloads or EMA bounces, particularly when paired with volume and RSI confirmation.

Liquidity Zone

Strategic areas where institutions accumulate or distribute. Often disguised as support or resistance, these zones are structured using coiling, emotional traps, and EMA wicks.

RSI (Relative Strength Index)

A momentum oscillator used across multiple timeframes. I use RSI baselines, divergence, and compression to detect wave energy. RSI must remain elevated or consolidate above key levels (50, 60, 70) to validate entries.

RSI Baseline

The moving average of RSI. I often require price to remain near or above the RSI base before entry. A failure to reach it during coil formation suggests weak conviction.

Stacked Coil

An advanced coil setup with multiple overlapping EMAs compressing tightly. This is my strongest coil structure and most explosive when it breaks.

Stop Loss

Tactical risk control placed below coil lows or wick bottoms. My system avoids vague exits—each entry has a precise, predefined risk anchored to the structure.

Structural Wave

A wave that aligns across timeframes with confirmed energy. Wave 3 is the most explosive structural wave; Wave 5 is the redemption or trap wave. Both require confluence for entry.

VWAP (Volume-Weighted Average Price)

Used as a dynamic support level and psychological reference point. A key element in coil compression and bounce entries.

Wave 1 – Blueprint Reveal

The shallow first move that reveals institutional intent. Not typically traded, but studied for confirmation of early structure.

Wave 2 – The Trap

Pullback after Wave 1, typically into the 9 EMA. Emotional trap zone where smart money reloads and retail gets shaken out.

Wave 3 – Structural Release

My primary A+ entry wave. High-conviction momentum. Requires full energy stack, multi-timeframe RSI strength, and EMA alignment. I look for coil bounces and clean risk zones here off the 1-Min Time Frame along the 21 EMA.

Wave 4 – Distribution Coil

A stall or fakeout zone often designed to shake out late longs. Can lead to either continuation (Wave 5) or reversal.

Wave 5 – Redemption or Trap

Final push after consolidation. Can mimic Wave 3 but typically has less volume. Requires careful confirmation to avoid being baited into the final trap.

Wick Entry

A precise entry tactic using long lower wicks that tap into the EMA or liquidity zone. Must be paired with RSI baselining and volume spike.

Additional Relevant Financial/Trading Terms

Accumulation

A period where smart money (institutions) slowly buy shares without significantly moving price. Often seen during coil phases or before Wave 1 begins.

Algorithmic Forces / High-Frequency Trading (HFT)

Refers to automated trading systems that execute trades in milliseconds. These can help "builders" push price when EMA alignments are triggered.

Backtesting

A method of validating a strategy by replaying historical chart data. My book uses replay mode in TradingView to test entries and log statistics.

Breakout

A move above resistance or below support, often initiating a new wave. My system distinguishes real breakouts (with energy stack + volume) from fakeouts.

Candle / Candlestick

A single bar on a chart that shows open, high, low, and close. Candle shape (e.g., hammer, doji) is used for timing and confirmation.

Chart Timeframes

Intervals at which price data is aggregated. My book emphasizes multi-timeframe analysis: 1-min, 5-min, 15-min, and 30-min.

Confluence

The overlap of multiple signals (RSI, ADX, EMA, Volume, Price Action) that validate a trade. I prioritize confluence as a non-negotiable entry rule.

Distribution

The process of institutions offloading shares into retail strength—often masked by sideways coils or slow uptrends in Wave 4 and 5.

Entry Trigger

The specific technical and psychological moment to enter a trade. In your system, it's often the touch of a compressed EMA during a coil with rising volume and RSI alignment.

Exhaustion Candle

A large, emotionally driven candle (usually with volume spike) marking the end of a move. If seen on Wave 5 without confirmation, it's a trap.

Fake Breakdown

A candle or wick that dips below support or an EMA to scare out weak hands—only to reverse violently upward. A common institution tactic.

Hammer Candle

A bullish reversal candle with a long lower wick and small body. Used in my strategy to signal coil reloads or confirmation near EMAs.

Liquidity

The ease with which a stock can be bought or sold without moving price. My framework treats volume as fuel and liquidity zones as construction sites for waves.

Momentum

The rate of price acceleration. I measure this through RSI and ADX, especially when aligning Wave 3 or confirming a 5th wave continuation.

Retest

When price revisits a prior level (e.g., EMA or VWAP) after an initial move. In my execution rules, retests are safer entries than chases.

Risk-Reward Ratio

The potential profit compared to the risk (distance to stop-loss). Implied in my entry rules, where tight coils offer low-risk, high-reward trades.

Scalping

Quick, short-term trades typically based on 1-min or 5-min charts. My system supports scalping when coil compression and energy stack align perfectly.

Support / Resistance

Price levels where buying or selling pressure historically reverses price. In my framework, these levels are often EMAs or VWAP—not just static lines.

Trend Alignment

The requirement that higher and lower timeframes are all showing momentum in the same direction. If misaligned, my strategy voids the trade.

Made in United States
Troutdale, OR
07/30/2025